SPECTRUM®

Word Problems

Grade 2

Spectrum®
An imprint of Carson Dellosa Education
Greensboro, North Carolina

Spectrum®
An imprint of Carson Dellosa Education
P.O. Box 35665
Greensboro, NC 27425 USA

Printed in the USA • All rights reserved.   ISBN 978-1-4838-0439-2

01-279207784

Table of Contents Grade 2

Table of Contents, continued

Lesson 2.5 Odd and Even Numbers Practice

Read the problem carefully and solve.
Show your work under each question.

The chart shows how many pets are at Ming's pet store.

Cats	9
Dogs	7
Rabbits	8
Fish	14

Helpful Hint

Adding an odd and an even number always gives you an odd sum.

1. How many cats and dogs are there altogether?

   _____ cats and dogs

2. How many rabbits and fish are there altogether?

   _____ rabbits and fish

3. Ming added 6 more cats. How many cats does he have altogether?

   _____ cats

Check What You Learned

Working with Equal Groups of Objects

Read the problem carefully and solve. Show your work under each question.

Tony has 8 packs of note cards. Each pack has 6 cards.

1. How many note cards does Tony have altogether?

_____ note cards

3. How many note cards does Tony have if he counts his old note cards and his new note cards?

_____ note cards

2. If Tony buys 3 more packs of note cards, how many new cards does he have?

_____ note cards

4. Kim has 4 packs of note cards. Each pack has 5 note cards. How many note cards does Kim have altogether?

_____ note cards

Check What You Know

Understanding Place Value

Read the problem carefully and solve. Show your work under each question.

Billy went to a basketball game. The home team scored 102 points. The visitors scored 97 points.

1. In the number 102, which number is in the ones place?

_____

3. In the number 102, which number is in the hundreds place?

_____

2. In the number 97, which number is in the tens place?

_____

4. In the number 97, which number is in the ones place?

_____

Lesson 3.1 Understanding Place Value to Ones

Read the problem carefully and solve.
Show your work under each question.

José is counting the votes in the class election. The chart shows the number of votes each student received.

Freddy	142
Marcus	99
Mira	117
Ashley	123

Helpful Hint

When you write a number in expanded form, you can see the value of each place.

147 = 100 + 40 + 7

1. José wants to use expanded form to write Mira's total number of votes. How is 107 written in expanded form?

_____

2. What is the value of the ones place in Freddy's total number of votes?

_____

3. Which student has the highest number in the ones place? What is the value of that number?

_____ has the highest number. The value of that number is _____.

NAME _____

Lesson 3.2 Understanding Place Value to Tens

Read the problem carefully and solve. Show your work under each question.

Hannah is buying glasses for her store. She needs 38 red glasses, 52 blue glasses, and 14 green glasses.

Helpful Hint

The value of the number in the tens place is the digit multiplied by 10. You can find this number by adding a 0 to the digit.

In the number 82, adding a 0 to the 8 in the tens place tells you its value is 80.

1. What is the value of the 3 in the number 38?

_____

2. What number is in the tens place in the number of blue glasses?

_____

3. What is the value of the tens digit in the number 14?

_____

Lesson 3.3 Understanding Place Value to Hundreds

Read the problem carefully and solve. Show your work under each question.

Nina is sorting books at the library. She has 236 picture books. She has 120 paperback books. She has 489 hardcover books.

Helpful Hint

Place values always go from highest to lowest. In a 3-digit number, the hundreds place is on the left. The tens place is in the middle. The ones place is on the right.

1. What is the value of the 2 in the number 236?

_____

2. What number is in the hundreds place in the number of paperback books?

_____

3. Which number has the highest value in the hundreds place?

_____

Lesson 3.4 Understanding Place Value in 100–900

Read the problem carefully and solve. Show your work under each question.

Caro is counting beads. She knows there are 100 beads in each box. She has 9 boxes of beads.

> **Helpful Hint**
>
> You can count by 100 like this: one hundred, two hundred, three hundred, and so on.

1. How many beads does Caro have altogether?

_____ beads

2. If Caro counts 4 boxes, how many beads does she have?

_____ beads

3. What is the value of the 7 in the number 700?

_____

Lesson 3.5 Skip Counting by 5s, 10s, and 100s

Read the problem carefully and solve. Show your work under each question.

Chen is counting buttons. He puts the buttons in groups to count them.

Helpful Hint

Skip counting makes it easier to count large groups of objects.

1. Chen puts the black buttons in groups of 5. He has 6 groups of black buttons. How many black buttons does he have?

_____ black buttons

2. Chen puts the brown buttons in groups of 10. He has 4 groups of brown buttons. How many brown buttons does he have?

_____ brown buttons

3. Chen puts the white buttons in groups of 100. He has 5 groups of white buttons. How many white buttons does he have?

_____ white buttons

Lesson 3.6 Place Value Practice

Read the problem carefully and solve. Show your work under each question.

Henry is counting the number of cans his school recycled. The chart shows the number of cans recycled by each grade.

Grade 1	332 Cans
Grade 2	114 Cans
Grade 3	107 Cans
Grade 4	259 Cans
Grade 5	280 Cans

Helpful Hint

The digit 0 means there are no numbers in that place value.

1. Which grade has the highest number in the ones place? What is that number?

   Grade _____ has the highest number in the ones place.

   That number is _____.

2. Which grade has the highest number in the tens place? What is that number?

   Grade _____ has the highest number in the tens place.

   That number is _____.

3. Which grade has the highest number in the hundreds place? What is that number?

   Grade _____ has the highest number in the hundreds place.

   That number is _____.

NAME _____

 Check What You Learned

Understanding Place Value

Read the problem carefully and solve. Show your work under each question.

Carlos and Juan are making sandwiches. Carlos makes 152 turkey sandwiches. Juan makes 208 cheese sandwiches.

1. How would you write the number of sandwiches Carlos made if you are writing the number in expanded form?

_____

2. Which boy made sandwiches with the smallest number in the tens place? What is that number?

_____ made the sandwiches with the smallest number in the tens place.

That number is _____.

3. Carlos wants to make 10 more sandwiches. If he uses 2 slices of bread for each sandwich, how many slices of bread does he need?

_____ slices of bread

4. Which boy made sandwiches with the biggest number in the hundreds place? What is that number?

_____ made the sandwiches with the biggest number in the hundreds place.

That number is _____.

Spectrum Word Problems
Grade 2
22

Check What You Learned
Chapter 3

Check What You Know

Reading and Writing Numbers to 1,000

Read the problem carefully and solve. Show your work under each question.

Nelli is writing a report about her city. She finds out that there are 52 schools in her city. There are 1,454 houses. There are 123 stores.

---

1. How can Nelli write the number of stores in her city if she is writing the number in expanded form?

_____ stores

3. In the number 1,454, what number is in the thousands place?

_____

2. Are there more schools or more stores in Nelli's city?

Use the symbol <, >, or = to compare the 2 numbers.

52 _____ 123

4. In the number 52, what number is in the ones place?

_____

Lesson 4.1 Reading and Writing Numbers Using Numerals

Read the problem carefully and solve. Show your work under each question.

There are three hundred eighty-three students in Melissa's school. There are four hundred nineteen students in George's school.

Helpful Hint

Each number word or phrase can be represented by a numeral.

One thousand five hundred thirty-seven

1,000   500   30   7

1,537

1. Using numerals, write the number of students in Melissa's school.

_____ students

2. Using numerals, write the number of students in George's school.

_____ students

3. Whose school has the greater number of students?

_____'s school

Lesson 4.2 Reading and Writing Numbers Using Expanded Form

Read the problem carefully and solve. Show your work under each question.

Mr. Smith's class read a total of 1,283 pages.

Mrs. Albin's class read a total of 837 pages.

Helpful Hint

Writing a number in expanded form helps you see the value of each place.

$2,000 + 300 + 60 + 4 =$

    2 thousands
    3 hundreds
    6 tens
    4 ones

    2,364

2. How would you write the number of pages Mrs. Albin's class read if you are writing the number in expanded form?

_____

1. How would you write the number of pages Mr. Smith's class read if you are writing the number in expanded form?

_____

3. Which class read more pages?

_____

Lesson 4.3 Using <, >, and =

Read the problem carefully and solve. Show your work under each question.

Sammy is counting how many cars drive down Main Street. On Monday, he counted 1,038 cars. On Tuesday, he counted 684 cars. On Wednesday, he counted 469 cars. On Thursday, he counted 684 cars.

Helpful Hint

The smaller part of the symbol always points toward the number that is less.

The larger part of the symbol always points toward the number that is greater.

< means less than

> means greater than

2. Did Sammy count more cars on Wednesday or Thursday? Use the symbol <, >, or = to compare the 2 numbers.

469 _____ 684

1. Did Sammy count more cars on Monday or Tuesday? Use the symbol <, >, or = to compare the 2 numbers.

1,038 _____ 684

3. Did Sammy count more cars on Tuesday or Thursday? Use the symbol <, >, or = to compare the 2 numbers.

684 _____ 684

Lesson 4.4 Reading and Writing Numbers Practice

Read the problem carefully and solve. Show your work under each question.

Brendan has 485 paper clips. Tamika has 798 paper clips. Marissa has 652 paper clips.

Helpful Hint

Looking at the numerals in the highest place value can tell you if a number is greater than or less than another number.

2,631 > 1,857

1. How would you write the number of Brendan's paper clips if you are writing the number in expanded form?

_____

2. What numeral is in the hundreds place in the number of Tamika's paper clips?

_____

3. Who has more paper clips, Brendan or Marissa? Use the symbol <, >, or = to compare the 2 numbers.

485 _____ 652

_____ has more paper clips.

Check What You Learned

Reading and Writing Numbers to 1,000

Read the problem carefully and solve. Show your work under each question.

Dora's class and her sister Teresa's class had a jumping jack contest. Dora's class did 1,037 jumping jacks. Teresa's class did 1,142 jumping jacks.

1. What numeral is in the thousands place in both numbers?

_____

3. Whose class did more jumping jacks? Use <, >, or = to compare the 2 numbers.

1,037 _____1,142

2. How would you write the number of jumping jacks Dora's class did if you are writing the number in expanded form?

_____

4. Rita's class did two thousand three hundred fourteen jumping jacks. How would you write that number using numerals?

_____

NAME _____

Check What You Know

CHAPTER 5 PRETEST

Adding and Subtracting Using Place Value

Read the problem carefully and solve. Show your work under each question.

Sarita and her father are making cookies for a party. They make 452 peanut butter cookies. They make 276 chocolate chip cookies. They make 651 sugar cookies.

1. How many peanut butter and chocolate chip cookies do they have altogether?

_____ cookies

3. How many more peanut butter cookies than chocolate chip cookies do they have?

_____ cookies

2. How many more sugar cookies than peanut butter cookies do they have?

_____ cookies

4. They make 123 more chocolate chip cookies. How many chocolate chip cookies do they have altogether?

_____ cookies

Lesson 5.1 Adding 2-Digit Numbers

Read the problem carefully and solve. Show your work under each question.

Gabe is building with blocks. He has 35 red blocks. He has 28 blue blocks. He has 23 white blocks. He has 67 green blocks.

Helpful Hint

To add 2-digit numbers, first add the ones. Then add the tens.

1. How many red blocks and white blocks does Gabe have altogether?

   _____ blocks

2. How many blue blocks and green blocks does Gabe have altogether?

   _____ blocks

3. Gabe uses all the blue blocks and white blocks to build a house. How many blocks does he use?

   _____ blocks

Lesson 5.2 Subtracting 2-Digit Numbers

Read the problem carefully and solve. Show your work under each question.

Don has 52 pencils and 24 pens. Maria has 36 pencils and 28 pens.

Helpful Hint

To find how many fewer pencils or pens Don and Maria have, subtract the smaller number from the larger number.

1. How many more pencils does Don have than Maria?

_____ pencils

2. If Maria gives 12 pencils to Don, how many pencils does she have left?

_____ pencils

3. If Don gives 6 pens to Maria, how many pens does he have left?

_____ pens

Lesson 5.3 Adding 3-Digit Numbers

Read the problem carefully and solve. Show your work under each question.

Jan works at a food store. Jan puts 126 boxes of cereal on the shelves. She puts 345 boxes of cookies on the shelves. She puts 458 cans of soup on the shelves.

Helpful Hint

To add 3-digit numbers:

1. Add the ones first.

2. Add the tens next.

3. Add the hundreds last.

4. Carry any number from right to left.

$$\begin{array}{r} \overset{1}{4}25 \\ + 237 \\ \hline 662 \end{array}$$

1. How many boxes of cereal and boxes of cookies does Jan put on the shelves altogether?

_____ boxes

2. How many boxes of cookies and cans of soup does Jan put on the shelves altogether?

_____ boxes and cans

3. Jan puts 148 more boxes of cereal on the shelves. How many boxes of cereal does she put on the shelves altogether?

_____ boxes

Lesson 5.4 Subtracting 3-Digit Numbers

Read the problem carefully and solve. Show your work under each question.

Judy is selling lemonade for the drama club. She has 438 cups of lemonade to sell.

Helpful Hint

To subtract 3-digit numbers:

1. Subtract the ones first.

2. Subtract the tens next.

3. Subtract the hundreds last.

$$
\begin{array}{r}
269 \\
-\ 116 \\
\hline
153
\end{array}
$$

1. Mr. Drummond buys 112 cups of lemonade for his students. How many cups does Judy have left?

_____ cups

2. Then, Ms. Anderson buys 125 cups of lemonade for her students. How many cups does Judy have left now?

_____ cups

3. Then, Mr. We buys 201 cups of lemonade for his students. How many cups does Judy have left now?

_____ cups

Lesson 5.5 Adding and Subtracting Practice

Read the problem carefully and solve. Show your work under each question.

Lily and Susan are playing video games. Lily scores 158 points. Susan scores 367 points.

Helpful Hint

Remember to regroup if the digit above is less than the digit below.

$$
\begin{array}{r}
{\scriptstyle 3\ 11\ 13} \\
\cancel{4}\cancel{2}\cancel{3} \\
-\ 287 \\
\hline
1\,36
\end{array}
$$

1. How many points did Lily and Susan score altogether?

_____ points

2. How many more points did Susan score than Lily?

_____ points

3. Lily played again and scored 74 points. How many points does Lily have in both games?

_____ points

NAME _____

 Check What You Learned

Adding and Subtracting Using Place Value

Read the problem carefully and solve. Show your work under each question.

Chloe's store has 258 shirts, 357 pants, 184 dresses, and 165 hats.

1. How many shirts and pants does Chloe have altogether?

   _____ shirts and pants

3. Then, Chloe gets 37 more hats. How many hats does she have altogether?

   _____ hats

2. Chloe sells 52 dresses. How many dresses does she have left?

   _____ dresses

4. Next, Chloe sells 138 shirts. How many shirts does she have left?

   _____ shirts

Check What You Know

Adding and Subtracting More Than Two Numbers

Read the problem carefully and solve. Show your work under each question.

Isabel is counting flowers in the garden. She counts 52 red flowers, 36 white flowers, 28 blue flowers, and 77 yellow flowers.

1. How many red, white, and blue flowers does Isabel count altogether?

   _____ flowers

2. How many red, white, blue, and yellow flowers does Isabel count altogether?

   _____ flowers

3. Isabel picks 8 red flowers. Her sister picks 13 red flowers. How many red flowers are left?

   _____ red flowers

4. Isabel picks 17 white flowers. Her sister picks 9 white flowers. How many white flowers are left?

   _____ white flowers

Lesson 6.1 Adding Three Numbers (1- and 2-Digit)

Read the problem carefully and solve. Show your work under each question.

This chart shows how many points Rachel, Esti, and Shana scored in 3 basketball games.

Player	Game #1	Game #2	Game #3
Rachel	14	8	17
Esti	18	11	23
Shana	9	6	14

Helpful Hint

To add three 2-digit numbers, stack the numbers to set up the addition problem. Add the ones first. Then add the tens.

1. How many total points did Rachel score in all 3 games?

_____ points

2. How many total points did Esti score in all 3 games?

_____ points

3. How many points did Rachel, Esti, and Shana score altogether in game #3?

_____ points

Lesson 6.2 Subtracting Three Numbers (1- and 2-Digit)

Read the problem carefully and solve. Show your work under each question.

Sanjay is taking photos. He has 48 photos of trees. He has 37 photos of cars. He has 24 photos of birds.

Helpful Hint

When subtracting, be careful to line up the numbers correctly so the place value lines up.

$$
\begin{array}{r}
49 \\
26 \\
-\ 12 \\
\hline
11
\end{array}
$$

1. Howard buys 13 of Sanjay's tree photos. Lucy buys 18 tree photos. How many tree photos does Sanjay have left?

_____ tree photos

2. Then, Lucas buys 6 of Sanjay's bird photos. The next day, he buys 10 more bird photos. How many bird photos does Sanjay have left?

_____ bird photos

3. On Thursday, Sanjay sells 5 car photos. On Friday, he sells 12 car photos. How many car photos does Sanjay have left?

_____ car photos

Lesson 6.3 Adding Four Numbers (2-Digit)

Read the problem carefully and solve. Show your work under each question.

Mr. Watkin sells fruit. On Monday, he sold 14 apples and 23 peaches. On Tuesday, he sold 10 apples and 15 peaches. On Wednesday, he sold 24 apples and 37 peaches. On Thursday, he sold 38 apples and 43 peaches.

Helpful Hint

You can make the addition of 3 or more numbers easier by adding 2 of the numbers first, and then adding the other numbers to the total.

1. How many apples did Mr. Watkin sell altogether?

   _____ apples

2. How many peaches did Mr. Watkin sell altogether?

   _____ peaches

3. Mr. Watkin also sold 23 oranges on Monday, 16 oranges on Tuesday, 47 oranges on Wednesday, and 34 oranges on Thursday. How many oranges did Mr. Watkin sell altogether?

   _____ oranges

Lesson 6.4 Subtracting Four Numbers (2-Digit)

Read the problem carefully and solve. Show your work under each question.

Justin planted 97 tomato plants. Lindsay planted 84 tomato plants. This chart shows how many tomato plants Justin and Lindsay planted this week.

	Monday	Tuesday	Wednesday	Thursday
Justin	27	14	18	31
Lindsay	31	12	21	11

Helpful Hint

To subtract more than one number, keep a running total as you work.

$$
\begin{array}{r}
99 \\
- 31 \\
\hline
68 \\
- 32 \\
\hline
36 \\
- 15 \\
\hline
21 \\
- 10 \\
\hline
11
\end{array}
$$

1. How many tomato plants does Justin have left to plant at the end of the week?

_____ plants

2. How many tomato plants does Lindsay have left to plant at the end of the week?

_____ plants

3. Justin and Lindsay's mom had 54 tomato plants to plant. She planted 11 plants every day from Monday to Thursday. How many tomato plants did she have left to plant at the end of the week?

_____ plants

Lesson 6.5 Addition and Subtraction Practice

Read the problem carefully and solve. Show your work under each question.

Ella's Ice Cream Store sells vanilla, chocolate, strawberry, and mint chocolate chip ice cream cones.

Helpful Hint

To subtract more than 1 number, sometimes it is easier to add up all the numbers and subtract the total.

1. On Monday, Ella sold 14 vanilla cones, 35 chocolate cones, 27 strawberry cones, and 12 mint chocolate chip cones. How many cones did she sell altogether?

   _____ cones

2. On Tuesday, Ella sold 13 vanilla cones, 38 chocolate cones, 43 strawberry cones, and 0 mint chocolate chip cones. How many cones did she sell altogether?

   _____ cones

3. Ella made 99 ice cream cones on Thursday. She sold 25 vanilla cones, 21 chocolate cones, 17 strawberry cones, and 12 mint chocolate chip cones. How many cones did she have left?

   _____ cones

Check What You Learned

Adding and Subtracting More Than Two Numbers

Read the problem carefully and solve. Show your work under each question.

Reggie sells maps. He has 50 maps of New York, 62 maps of Florida, and 45 maps of California.

1. How many maps does Reggie have altogether?

_____ maps

2. Then, Reggie gets 47 maps of Maine. Now how many maps does he have altogether?

_____ maps

3. Next, Reggie sells a lot of Florida maps this week. He sells 11 on Monday, 17 on Tuesday, and 14 on Wednesday. How many Florida maps does he have left?

_____ maps

4. Then, Reggie sells 14 maps of Maine on Monday, 10 on Tuesday, 11 on Wednesday, and 12 on Thursday. Does he have any Maine maps left at the end of the week?

_____

Check What You Know

Adding By Tens and Hundreds

Read the problem carefully and solve. Show your work under each question.

Javi is bird-watching. He sees 10 robins, 10 blue jays, 10 finches, and 10 crows.

1. How many birds does Javi see altogether?

   _____ birds

2. Javi's father has seen 100 robins, 100 blue jays, 100 finches, 100 crows, and 100 doves this month. How many birds has he seen altogether?

   _____ birds

3. Javi sees 10 more robins. How many robins has he seen altogether?

   _____ robins

4. Javi's father sees 127 blue jays in May and 100 more in June. How many blue jays has he seen altogether?

   _____ blue jays

NAME _____

Lesson 7.1 Adding by Tens

Read the problem carefully and solve. Show your work under each question.

Meg is picking corn. She picks 10 ears of corn in the first row, 10 ears in the second row, 10 ears in the third row, and 10 ears in the fourth row.

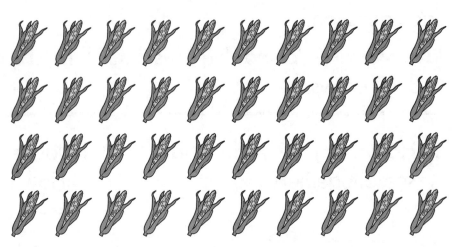

Helpful Hint

When you add by tens, the number in the ones place stays the same and the number in the tens place goes up by 1.

$$\begin{array}{r} 60 \\ +\ 10 \\ \hline 70 \end{array}$$

1. How many ears of corn does Meg pick in the first three rows?

_____ ears

2. How many ears of corn did Meg pick altogether?

_____ ears

3. If Meg picks 10 more ears of corn, how many ears will she have altogether?

_____ ears

Lesson 7.2 Adding by Hundreds

Read the problem carefully and solve. Show your work under each question.

Mr. Martin did 100 pushups every day of the week.

Helpful Hint

When you add by hundreds, the number in the ones place and the number in the tens place stay the same, and the number in the hundreds place goes up by 1.

$$
\begin{array}{r}
800 \\
+ \ 100 \\
\hline
900
\end{array}
$$

1. How many pushups did Mr. Martin do on Monday and Tuesday?

_____ pushups

2. How many pushups did Mr. Martin do on Monday, Tuesday, and Wednesday?

_____ pushups

3. Mr. Martin did 700 pushups this week. If he does 100 more pushups, how many pushups will he have done altogether?

_____ pushups

Lesson 7.3 Adding by Tens and Hundreds Practice

Read the problem carefully and solve. Show your work under each question.

Tamba collects rocks. He has striped rocks, black rocks, red rocks, and white rocks.

Helpful Hint

When you count by 10s and 100s, only the number in the tens or hundreds place changes.

1. If Tamba has 10 of each kind of rock, how many rocks does he have?

   _____ rocks

2. If Tamba has 100 of each kind of rock, how many rocks does he have?

   _____ rocks

3. Tamba has 50 flat rocks and 200 curved rocks. He finds 10 more flat rocks and 10 more curved rocks. How many of each kind of rock does he have?

   _____ flat rocks

   _____ curved rocks

Check What You Learned

Adding By Tens and Hundreds

Read the problem carefully and solve. Show your work under each question.

Corey is stacking boxes. She puts 10 boxes in each stack.

1. Corey makes 6 stacks of boxes. How many boxes does she have?

_____ boxes

3. Next, Tomas moves Corey's boxes into groups of 100 boxes in each stack. Tomas has 8 stacks. How many boxes does Tomas have?

_____ boxes

2. Then, Corey makes 3 more stacks of boxes. How many boxes does she have altogether?

_____ boxes

4. Then, Tomas adds 100 more boxes. How many boxes does he have altogether?

_____ boxes

Mid-Test Chapters 1–7

Read the problem carefully and solve. Show your work under each question.

Lee is buying toys. He buys 16 toy trains, 14 dolls, 8 robots, and 8 games.

---

1. How many trains and robots does Lee have?

_____ trains and robots

3. Lee gives 5 robots to his friends. How many robots does Lee have left?

_____ robots

2. How many robots and games does Lee have?

_____ robots and games

4. Then, Lee gives 12 toy trains to his friends. How many trains does Lee have left?

_____ trains

Mid-Test Chapters 1–7

Read the problem carefully and solve. Show your work under each question.

Giana has 436 bottles. In her collection, 131 bottles are green, 100 bottles are brown, and 205 bottles are red.

---

1. What is the value of the number in the ones place in 436?

_____

2. What is the value of the number in the hundreds place in 205?

_____

3. How would you write the number of Giana's green bottles if you are writing the number in expanded form?

_____

4. Does Giana have more brown bottles or more red bottles? Use <, >, or =.

100 _____ 205

Mid-Test Chapters 1–7

Read the problem carefully and solve. Show your work under each question.

Barry's Sports Store has 52 baseballs, 37 basketballs, 85 footballs, and 76 soccer balls.

---

1. How many baseballs and basketballs does the store have?

_____ balls

2. How many footballs and soccer balls does the store have?

_____ balls

3. Barry sold 15 basketballs. How many basketballs does the store have left?

_____ basketballs

4. Then, Barry sold 45 soccer balls. How many soccer balls does the store have left?

_____ soccer balls

Mid-Test Chapters 1–7

Read the problem carefully and solve. Show your work under each question.

This chart shows how many students ride buses to school.

Bus #1	15
Bus #2	22
Bus #3	27
Bus #4	18

1. How many students ride Bus #1, Bus #2, and Bus #3 altogether?

   _____ students

2. How many students ride all 4 buses?

   _____ students

3. On Wednesday, 5 students did not ride Bus #3. On Thursday, 3 more students did not ride Bus #3. On Friday, 11 more students did not ride Bus #3. How many students were on the bus on Friday?

   _____ students

4. There were 10 more students who rode Bus #4 on Thursday. Then, 10 more students rode Bus #4 on Friday. How many students were on Bus #4 on Friday?

   _____ students

Check What You Know

Measuring and Estimating Lengths

Read the problem carefully and solve. Show your work under each question.

Terri wants to put school supplies in her new desk. She measures each item to see if it will fit.

---

1. How long is Terri's pencil? Use a ruler to find the length to the nearest inch.

_____ inches

2. Terri has 3 erasers. Each eraser is 5 inches long. How long are the erasers altogether?

_____ inches

3. How long is Terri's crayon? Use a ruler to find the length to the nearest inch.

_____ inches

4. Terri wants to measure her desk. Would her desk be 2 feet wide or 20 feet wide?

_____ feet

Lesson 8.1   Using Tools to Measure Lengths

Read the problem carefully and solve. Show your work under each question.

Frank cleans his room. He wants to measure several of the objects he finds in his room to the nearest inch.

> **Helpful Hint**
>
> To measure to the nearest inch, line your ruler up below the object. Measure the object, rounding to the closest whole number.

1. What is the length of the crayon?

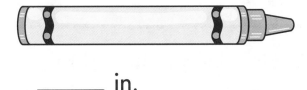

_____ in.

2. What is the length of the paper clip?

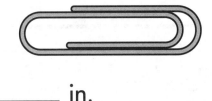

_____ in.

3. What is the length of the pencil?

_____ in.

Lesson 8.2 Using Different Length Units

Read the problem carefully and solve. Show your work under each question.

Marco is measuring fish in the aquarium.

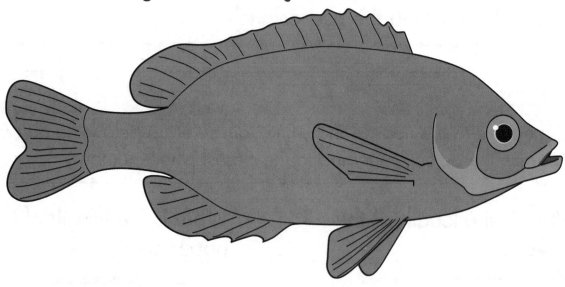

Helpful Hint

1 inch = 2.5 centimeters

36 inches = 3 feet

1 meter = 100 centimeters

1. How long is the red fish in inches? Use a ruler to find its length to the nearest inch.

_____ inches

2. How long is the red fish in centimeters? Use a ruler to find its length to the nearest centimeter.

_____ centimeters

3. Marco has to put the red fish in a new tank. Should he use a tank that is 3 feet long or a tank that is 3 centimeters long?

_____

Lesson 8.3 Estimating Lengths

Read the problem carefully and solve. Show your work under each question.

Matt is building a bookcase.

Helpful Hint

12 inches = 1 foot

3 feet   = 1 yard

1. Matt wants the bookcase to have 3 shelves. He wants each shelf to be 2 feet high. How many feet high will the bookcase be?

_____ feet

2. Each of Matt's books is 2 inches wide. If each shelf is 2 feet long, how many books can Matt fit on each shelf?

_____ books

3. Matt buys 12 more books. Each book is 4 inches wide. How many more shelves does Matt need to hold his new books if each shelf is 2 feet long?

_____ shelves

Lesson 8.4 Measuring and Estimating Practice

Read the problem carefully and solve. Show your work under each question.

Jada went to a street fair. She bought a skirt, a toy frog, and a doll.

Helpful Hint

Use a ruler to measure small objects. Use a yardstick or a measuring tape to measure larger objects.

1. Jada's skirt is 3 feet long. She wants it to be 24 inches long. How many inches should Jada cut off to make the skirt the right length?

_____ inches

2. How wide is Jada's toy frog? Use a ruler to find the length to the nearest inch.

_____ inches

3. Jada's doll is about 10 inches high. Will it fit on a shelf that is 1 foot tall?

_____

Check What You Learned

Measuring and Estimating Lengths

Read the problem carefully and solve. Show your work under each question.

Jorge and Will are measuring insects.

1. How long is this insect? Use a ruler to find the length to the nearest inch.

_____ inches

2. Will measures 2 insects. The fly is 1 inch long. The caterpillar is 1 centimeter long. Which insect is longer?

_____

3. Jorge finds some insects that are each 2 inches long. How many could fit on a branch that is 20 inches long?

_____ insects

4. Will draws a picture of his favorite butterfly. He wants to make the picture 1 yard wide. Should he measure the paper with a ruler or a measuring stick?

_____

Check What You Know

Measuring to Determine Longer and Shorter

Read the problem carefully and solve. Show your work under each question.

Robin is sewing a quilt. She buys 5 yards of blue cloth. She buys 3 yards of red cloth. She buys 8 yards of yellow cloth.

1. How many feet of cloth does Robin have altogether?

_____ feet

2. Robin buys 6 more yards of blue cloth. Now how much blue cloth does she have altogether?

_____ yards

3. Robin gives Flora 36 inches of yellow cloth. How many yards of yellow cloth does Robin have left?

_____ yards

4. Robin needs to have 10 yards of red cloth altogether. How many more yards should she buy?

_____ yards

Lesson 9.1 Using Addition to Solve Word Problems

Read the problem carefully and solve. Show your work under each question.

This chart shows how many feet Mari, Garret, and Joseph threw a ball in 3 tries.

Player	Try #1	Try #2	Try #3
Mari	5	8	7
Garret	6	7	2
Joseph	3	4	9

Helpful Hint

Each student's numbers can be found if you read across the rows on the chart. The numbers for each try can be found if you read down each column.

2. How many total feet did Joseph throw the ball?

_____ feet

1. How many total feet did Garret throw the ball in his 3 tries?

_____ feet

3. How many more feet does Mari need to throw the ball on her fourth try to throw it 27 feet altogether?

_____ feet

Lesson 9.2 Using Subtraction to Solve Word Problems

Read the problem carefully and solve. Show your work under each question.

Austin is hanging posters in his room. His wall is 4 feet long.

Helpful Hint

Remember to change feet into inches before solving these problems.

1. Austin hangs a car poster that is 24 inches long. How many inches does he have left on his wall?

_____ inches

2. Next, Austin hangs a tiger poster that is 16 inches long. Now how many inches does he have left on his wall?

_____ inches

3. Austin wants to hang a poster of the ocean. It is 10 inches long. Does Austin have enough room left on his wall to hang the poster?

_____

Lesson 9.3 Measuring Longer and Shorter Practice

Read the problem carefully and solve. Show your work under each question.

Chelsea has 4 toy trucks. The first truck measures 3 inches long. The second truck measures 6 inches long. The third truck measures 9 inches long. The fourth truck measures 13 inches long.

Helpful Hint

To see if all of the trucks will fit, first add the lengths together. Then subtract them from the size of the box.

1. How many inches long do Chelsea's trucks measure altogether?

_____ inches

2. Chelsea buys another toy truck that is 10 inches long. Now how many inches long do her trucks measure altogether?

_____ inches

3. Chelsea wants to put all 5 trucks in a box that is 4 feet long. How many inches will she have left over?

_____

Check What You Learned

Measuring to Determine Longer and Shorter

Read the problem carefully and solve. Show your work under each question.

Eddie has 3 teddy bears. The blue bear is 6 inches tall. The brown bear is 2 feet tall. The green bear is 15 inches tall.

1. How much taller is the brown bear than the green bear?

_____ inches

3. Eddie has a box that is 3 feet tall. If he puts the green bear inside, how many inches will he have left?

_____ inches

2. How many inches tall are the 3 bears altogether?

_____ inches

4. How tall are the brown bear and the blue bear altogether?

_____ inches

Check What You Know

Representing Lengths on a Number Line

Read the problem carefully and solve. Show your work under each question.

Alicia is plotting lengths on a number line.

1. Alicia's pen is 8 inches long. Plot that number on the number line.

2. Alicia has one eraser that is 3 inches long. Plot that number on the number line.

3. Alicia has a second eraser that is 4 inches long. How long are the 2 erasers altogether? Plot that number on the number line.

4. Alicia's pencil is 4 inches shorter than her pen. How long is her pencil? Plot that number on the number line.

Lesson 10.1 Finding Numbers on a Number Line

Read the problem carefully and solve.
Show your work under each question.

Ali has 5 photos. This chart shows
how long each photo is.

Cat Photo	10 inches
Dog Photo	15 inches
Bird Photo	5 inches
Fish Photo	25 inches
Lizard Photo	20 inches

Helpful Hint

When plotting on a number line, always count by the
same number between each point on the line.

1. Plot the length of the dog photo on the number line.

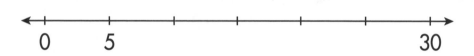

2. Plot the length of the fish photo on the number line.

3. Plot the length of the lizard photo on the number line.

Lesson 10.2 Representing Sums on a Number Line

Read the problem carefully and solve. Show your work under each question.

Shauna is making shirts. For each shirt, she needs 5 feet of cloth.

> **Helpful Hint**
>
> When you add on a number line, you always move to the right.

1. On Monday, Shauna made 3 shirts. How much cloth did she use? Plot the number on the number line.

2. On Tuesday, Shauna made 2 shirts. How much cloth did she use altogether on Monday and Tuesday? Plot the number on the number line.

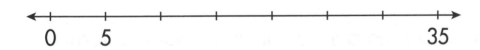

3. Shauna makes 1 more shirt. How much cloth did she use altogether for all 6 shirts? Plot the number on the number line.

Lesson 10.3 Representing Differences on a Number Line

Read the problem carefully and solve. Show your work under each question.

This chart shows how far Brandon's favorite race cars drove in a race.

Car	Distance
Black	50 miles
Red	70 miles
Purple	100 miles
Orange	30 miles

Helpful Hint

When you subtract on a number line, start with the larger number and move to the left on the number line.

1. How much farther did the black car drive than the orange car? Plot the number on the number line.

2. How much farther did the purple car drive than the red car? Plot the number on the number line.

3. What was the difference between how far the purple and orange cars drove? Plot the number on the number line.

Lesson 10.4 Number Line Practice

Read the problem carefully and solve. Show your work under each question.

Maryann, Liz, and Carmen went for a walk. Maryann walked 4 miles. Liz walked 8 miles. Carmen walked 6 miles.

> **Helpful Hint**
>
> Points on a number line always get larger or smaller by the same number.

1. How far did the 3 girls walk altogether? Plot the number on the number line.

2. How much farther did Liz walk than Maryann? Plot the number on the number line.

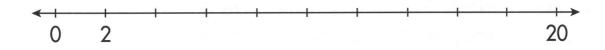

3. If Carmen walks 2 more miles, how many miles will she have walked altogether? Plot the number on the number line.

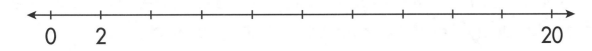

Check What You Learned

Representing Lengths on a Number Line

Read the problem carefully and solve. Show your work under each question.

Paul's family is on a long trip. On Monday, they drive 30 miles. On Tuesday, they drive 50 miles. On Wednesday, they drive 60 miles. On Thursday, they drive 40 miles.

1. How far does Paul's family drive altogether on Monday and Tuesday? Plot the number on the number line.

2. How far does Paul's family drive altogether on all 4 days? Plot the number on the number line.

3. How much farther did Paul's family drive on Wednesday than they did on Monday? Plot the number on the number line.

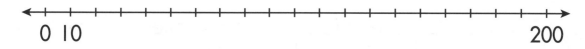

4. How much farther did Paul's family drive on Tuesday than they did on Monday? Plot the number on the number line.

Check What You Know

Measuring Lengths and Plotting Graphs

Read the problem carefully and solve. Show your work under each question.

Marina is growing flowers. She has 3 tulips. One is 4 inches tall and two are 6 inches tall. She has 4 daisies. Two are 7 inches tall and two are 8 inches tall. She also has 3 sunflowers. One is 12 inches tall, the second is 14 inches tall, and the third is 15 inches tall.

1. Plot the heights of Marina's flowers on the line plot.

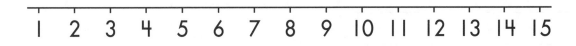

| 1 | 2 | 3 | 4 | 5 | 6 | 7 | 8 | 9 | 10 | 11 | 12 | 13 | 14 | 15 |

2. Plot the number of flowers on the picture graph.

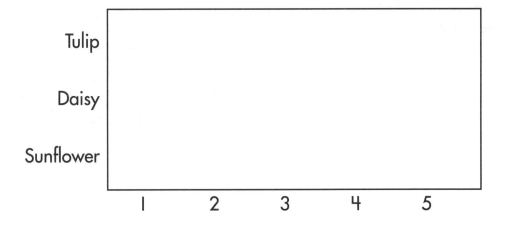

Check What You Know

Measuring Lengths and Plotting Graphs

Read the problem carefully and solve. Show your work under each question.

Marina picks some of her flowers. She picks one tulip that is 6 inches tall, one daisy that is 8 inches tall, and one sunflower that is 12 inches tall.

---

3. Plot the height of all 3 flowers on the bar graph.

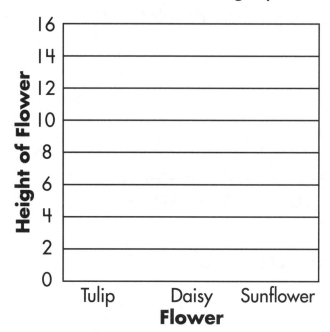

4. Marina replaces the sunflower with a sunflower that is 14 inches tall. Plot the new height on the bar graph.

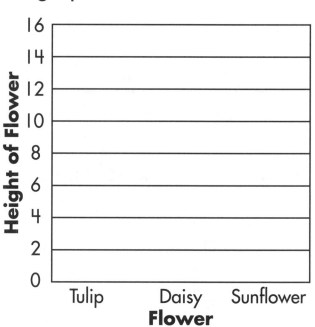

Lesson 11.1 Measuring and Making a Line Plot

Read the problem carefully and solve.
Show your work under each question.

Warren wants to know how many pets his friends have. He makes the chart to the right.

Eli	2 Pets
Damon	5 Pets
Irene	2 Pets
Ralph	1 Pet
Veronica	2 Pets
Lori	1 Pet

Helpful Hint

A line plot uses X's to mark the value of each number.

1. Plot the number of pets people have.

2. How many people have 1 pet?

_____ people

3. What is the most common number of pets people have?

_____

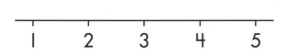

Lesson 11.2 Measuring and Making a Bar Graph

Read the problem carefully and solve. Show your work under each question.

Emily is counting the number of notebooks in the school store. The store has 10 red notebooks, 14 blue notebooks, 8 green notebooks, and 12 black notebooks.

Helpful Hint

You can use different colors for each bar to make them easier to see and read.

2. What color notebook does Emily count the most of?

_____

1. How many notebooks of each color does Emily count? Draw a bar on the graph to plot each number.

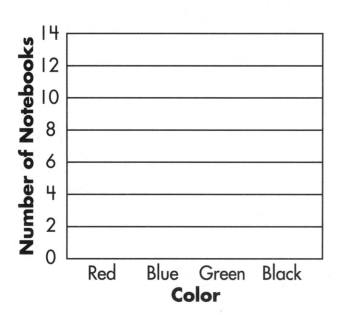

3. How many more black notebooks than green notebooks does Emily count?

_____ more

Lesson 11.3 Measuring and Making a Picture Graph

Read the problem carefully and solve. Show your work under each question.

Simon is making a graph to show how many different kinds of fruit he ate last week. He ate 4 apples, 10 cherries, 2 peaches, and 6 oranges.

> **Helpful Hint**
>
> Picture graphs use a symbol that represents each object being measured. So if you are showing 5 cakes, you would draw 5 cakes.

1. How many pieces of each fruit did Simon eat? Draw symbols on the picture graph to plot each number.

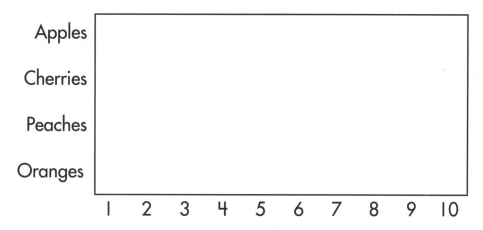

2. Which fruit did Simon eat the most of?

   _____

3. Simon ate 2 more peaches and 3 more apples. Add these fruits to the picture graph.

Lesson 11.4 Plotting Graphs Practice

Read the problem carefully and solve. Show your work under each question.

Kenny, Dorian, and Zane are cleaning the park. This chart shows what they found.

Kenny	20 Bottles, 4 Cans, 8 Plastic Bags
Dorian	5 Bottles, 8 Cans, 4 Plastic Bags
Zane	15 Bottles, 6 Cans, 3 Plastic Bags

Helpful Hint

Look at the numbers you need to include. Then, set the number range using the lowest common denominator for those numbers. For example, if your numbers are 5, 10, 20, and 25, you can make your graph count by 5s.

1. Draw a bar graph that shows how many bottles each boy collected.

Lesson 11.4 Plotting Graphs Practice (continued)

2. Draw a picture graph that shows how many cans each boy collected.

3. Draw a line plot to show how many bottles, cans, and plastic bags Dorian collected.

Check What You Learned

Measuring Lengths and Plotting Graphs

Read the problem carefully and solve. Show your work under each question.

Juan is building towers out of blocks. He builds one tower that is 5 inches high. He builds a second tower that is 8 inches high. He builds a third tower that is 10 inches high.

1. Draw a picture graph to show how high each tower is. Use blocks to represent inches.

2. Draw a bar graph to show how high each tower is.

Check What You Learned

Measuring Lengths and Plotting Graphs

Read the problem carefully and solve. Show your work under each question.

Juan divides his blocks up by color. He has one group of 7 blue blocks. He has another group of 5 orange blocks. He has another group of 12 purple blocks. He has another group of 3 green blocks.

1. Draw a line plot to show how many blocks of each color Juan has.

2. Draw a picture graph or bar graph that shows how many blocks of each color Juan has.

Check What You Know

Telling and Writing Time

Read the problem carefully and solve. Show your work under each question.

Eva is setting the clocks at her house.

1. What time does this clock show?

_____

2. What time does this clock show?

_____

3. Eva wants to set a digital clock to six o'clock. What numbers would the clock show?

_____

4. Eva adds 15 minutes to a digital clock that reads 3:45. What time does the clock show now?

_____

Lesson 12.1 Telling Time Using Analog Clocks

Read the problem carefully and solve. Show your work under each question.

Jack has many places to go today.

Helpful Hint

The small hand on an analog clock shows the hour. The big hand shows the minutes.

1. Jack has to be at school at eight o'clock. Show that time on the clock.

2. Jack is meeting his sister for lunch at eleven thirty. Show that time on the clock.

3. Jack has to go to the dentist at three twenty. Show that time on the clock.

Lesson 12.2 Telling Time Using Digital Clocks

Read the problem carefully and solve. Show your work under each question.

Padma is going to the movies.

Helpful Hint

The first number on a digital clock shows the hour. The next 2 numbers show the number of minutes past the hour.

1. The movie starts at eight o'clock. Show that time on the clock.

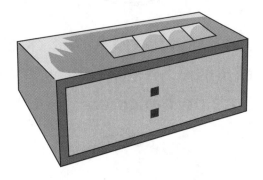

2. It takes Padma half an hour to get to the movie theater. What time should she leave to get to the theater at eight o'clock?

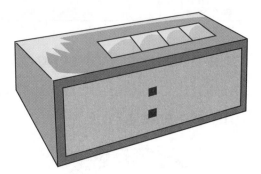

3. The movie lasts for 2 hours. What time will it be when the movie is over? Show that time on the clock.

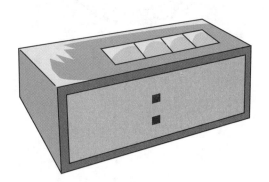

Lesson 12.3 Comparing Analog and Digital Clocks

Read the problem carefully and solve. Show your work under each question.

Cheryl is waiting for a bus at the bus station.

> **Helpful Hint**
>
> Analog clocks start each hour with the big hand on the 12. Digital clocks start each hour with the last 2 numbers showing 00.

1. The bus to New York leaves at one o'clock. Draw hands on the analog clock to show the time.

2. Cheryl's bus to Trenton leaves at two forty. Write the time on the digital clock.

3. Cheryl finds out that her bus will be 20 minutes late. What time will it arrive? Show the time on both clocks.

Lesson 12.4 Telling and Writing Time Practice

Read the problem carefully and solve. Show your work under each question.

Madison makes a list of her classes. She has science at 8:30. She has math at 9:00. She has history at 10:15.

Helpful Hint

Each space between the numbers on an analog clock represents 5 minutes when using the big hand and 1 hour when using the little hand.

1. Madison is 5 minutes late for science class. What time does she get to class?

2. Draw the time of Madison's math class on the digital clock.

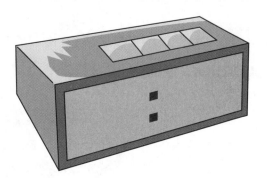

3. Which clock shows the time of Madison's history class?

_____ clock

Check What You Learned

Telling and Writing Time

Read the problem carefully and solve. Show your work under each question.

Philip is making a list of when his favorite team plays football. The team plays at 8:00 on Monday, 7:00 on Tuesday, 7:30 on Wednesday, and 8:20 on Thursday.

1. Draw the time of Monday's game on the analog clock.

2. Write the time of Tuesday's game on the digital clock.

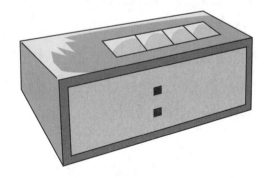

3. Wednesday's game starts 15 minutes late. Show the time the game starts on the digital clock.

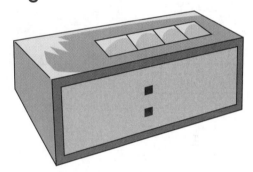

4. The team adds a game on Friday night. The game starts one hour past six o'clock. Show the time the game starts on both clocks.

NAME _____

Check What You Know

Solving Word Problems Involving Money

Read the problem carefully and solve. Show your work under each question.

Robert is at the supermarket. This chart shows the prices of the items he wants to buy.

Rice	$2.75
Cereal	$2.50
Milk	$3.45
Bag of Apples	$4.20

1. Robert buys one box of rice. How many dollars and quarters does he need to pay?

_____ dollars and

_____ quarters

2. Robert buys one bottle of milk and one bag of apples. How much does he spend?

_____

3. Robert buys one box of cereal. He gives the cashier $3.00. How much change does he get back?

_____ cents

4. Robert's total comes to $12.90. He gives the cashier a ten-dollar bill and a five-dollar bill. How much change does Robert get back?

_____ dollars and

_____ cents

Lesson 13.1 Money: Using Decimals

Read the problem carefully and solve. Show your work under each question.

Tim cleaned his room. As he cleaned his room, he collected any money he found and put it into a jar.

Helpful Hint

1 penny, 1 cent, 1¢, or $0.01
1 nickel, 5 cents, 5¢, or $0.05
1 dime, 10 cents, 10¢, or $0.10
1 quarter, 25 cents, 25¢, or $0.25
1 half dollar, 50 cents, 50¢, or $0.50
1 dollar, 100 cents, 100¢, or $1.00

1. Tim found 30 pennies under his bed. What is the value of 30 pennies in cents? How many nickels have the same value?

_____ cents   _____ nickels

2. Tim found 2 quarters in his dresser. What is the value of 2 quarters in cents? How many dimes have the same value?

_____ cents   _____ dimes

3. Tim found a total of $5.95 while cleaning his room. What is this amount written as dollars and cents?

_____ dollars   _____ cents

Lesson 13.2 Adding with Money

Read the problem carefully and solve. Show your work under each question.

Evan and Grace are earning money by doing chores.

Helpful Hint

The decimal point divides dollars and cents:

$2.50 equals 2 dollars and 50 cents

1. Evan has $2.20. He earns $1.50 for walking the dog. How much money does he have now?

_____ dollars and

_____ cents

2. Grace gets $1.00 for washing the dishes. She then gets $1.50 for drying the dishes and putting them away. How much money does Grace have?

_____ dollars and

_____ cents

3. Evan and Grace each get $3.50 for dusting the living room. Now how much money do they have?

Evan has _____ dollars and _____ cents

Grace has _____ dollars and _____ cents

Lesson 13.3 Subtracting with Money

Read the problem carefully and solve. Show your work under each question.

Adina has $20.00 that she will use to buy presents for her family.

Helpful Hint

When adding or subtracting money, stack the numbers and line up the decimal points. Then, subtract each column from right to left.

$$\begin{array}{r} \$6.26 \\ - \ \$4.10 \\ \hline \$2.16 \end{array}$$

1. Adina buys a picture for her mother. The picture costs $6.25. How much money does Adina have left? Write the answer using a decimal point.

   _____

2. Next, Adina buys a scarf for her father. The scarf costs $4.00. Now how much money does Adina have? Write the answer using a decimal point.

   _____

3. Next, Adina buys a book for her brother. The book costs $6.50. Now how much money does Adina have? Write the answer using a decimal point.

   _____

Lesson 13.4 Making Change

Read the problem carefully and solve. Show your work under each question.

Zahara works at her mom's jewelry store.

Helpful Hint

To find the change, subtract the cost of the item from the value of the money given to the cashier.

1. Zahara sells a ring to Mrs. Gorton. The ring costs $22.00. Mrs. Gorton gives Zahara $25.00. How much change does Zahara give Mrs. Gorton? Write the answer using a decimal point.

_____

2. Zahara sells 2 necklaces to Mr. Smith. Each necklace costs $35.00. Mr. Smith gives Zahara $100.00. How much change does Zahara give Mr. Smith? Write the answer using a decimal point.

_____

3. Ms. McDonald buys a bracelet that costs $16. She gives Zahara a twenty-dollar bill. How much change does Zahara give Ms. McDonald? Write the answer using a decimal point.

_____

NAME _____

Lesson 13.5 Money Practice

Read the problem carefully and solve. Show your work under each question.

Natasha has the money shown below.

Helpful Hint

To add different bills and coins, add the value of each group of similar bills and coins. Then add the numbers together.

1. How much money does Natasha have altogether?

_____ dollars and
_____ cents

2. Natasha's father gave her $4.00 to wash his car. Now how much money does she have? Write the answer using a decimal point.

_____

3. After she washed the car, Natasha spent $7.25 on snacks. She gave the cashier $10.00. How much change did Natasha get back? Write the answer using a decimal point.

_____

Check What You Learned

Solving Word Problems Involving Money

Read the problem carefully and solve. Show your work under each question.

Neil, Curtis, and Martin get $2.00 for every bag of cans they recycle.

---

1. On Saturday, Neil received the money shown below. How much money did he get? Write the answer using a decimal point.

_____

2. Curtis recycled 4 bags of cans. How much money did he get altogether? Write the answer using a decimal point.

_____

3. Martin earned $4.00. Later, he came back and earned $6.00 more. How much money did he earn altogether? Write the answer using a decimal point.

_____

4. The 3 boys earned $22.00 altogether. Then, they spent $4.00 on ice cream. How much change did they get back? Write the answer using a decimal point.

_____

NAME _____

Check What You Know

Recognizing and Drawing Shapes

Read the problem carefully and solve. Show your work under each question.

Eric is drawing shapes on the chalkboard.

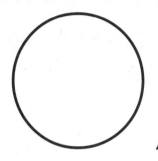   

1. Eric draws a triangle. Draw a triangle in the space below.

3. Eric draws a square. How many sides does it have?

_____

4. Eric draws a rectangle that is not a square. He divides it into 4 equal parts. Draw a rectangle divided into 4 equal parts in the space below.

2. Eric draws a circle. How many sides does a circle have?

_____

Lesson 14.1 Identifying Triangles

Read the problem carefully and solve. Show your work under each question.

Bonita is cutting out pieces of cloth for an art project. She cuts out pieces of different shapes.

Helpful Hint

The prefix *tri* means "three." So the word *triangle* means "three angles."

2. How many sides does a triangle have?

_____

1. Which of the following shapes is a triangle?

1.   2.   3.

3. How many angles does a triangle have?

_____

_____

NAME _____

Lesson 14.2 Identifying Quadrilaterals

Read the problem carefully and solve. Show your work under each question.

Sonya is covering a wall with different pieces of colored construction paper. All her pieces of construction paper are quadrilaterals.

Helpful Hint

A **quadrilateral** is a shape with 4 sides.

1. How many sides does each piece of construction paper have?

_____

2. Which of the following shapes is a quadrilateral?

   1.   2.   3.

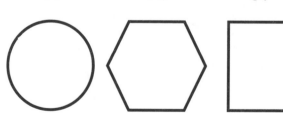

_____

3. Sonya wants to cover the wall using pieces of construction paper that have 4 sides with equal lengths. Should she choose pieces of construction paper that are squares or rectangles?

_____

Lesson 14.3 Identifying Pentagons and Hexagons

Read the problem carefully and solve. Show your work under each question.

Giacomo is cutting out pieces of construction paper. He wants to cut out shapes with 5 and 6 sides.

Helpful Hint

A **pentagon** has 5 sides.

A **hexagon** has 6 sides.

1. Which of these shapes has 6 sides?

1.   2.   3.

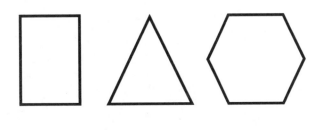

_____

2. How many angles does a pentagon have?

_____ angles

3. Giacomo cuts a piece of paper into the figure shown below. What is the name of this figure?

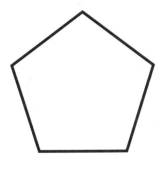

_____

Lesson 14.4 Identifying Cubes

Read the problem carefully and solve. Show your work under each question.

Noah is stacking cubes.

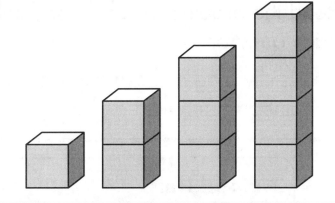

Helpful Hint

A **square** is a plane, or flat, figure. A **cube** is a solid figure. It has 3 dimensions.

1. How many faces, or sides, does each cube have?

_____ faces

2. How many angles does each face of the cube have?

_____ angles

3. What is the shape of each face of the cube?

_____

Lesson 14.5 Dividing Rectangles

Read the problem carefully and solve. Show your work under each question.

Zoe is dividing a rectangle-shaped box into smaller sections for her stuffed animals.

Helpful Hint

To divide a rectangle into equal sections, measure the length of the rectangle. Then, divide the rectangle into sections.

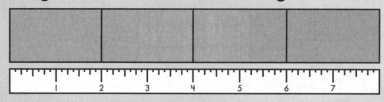

1. Zoe divides the rectangle into 3 equal sections. Show this in the space below.

2. Zoe wants to divide the rectangle into 4 equal sections instead of 3. Show this in the space below.

3. Zoe changes her mind again. She wants to divide the rectangle into 2 equal sections. Will each of these sections be bigger or smaller than the 4 equal sections she had before?

_____

Lesson 14.6 Dividing Circles

Read the problem carefully and solve. Show your work under each question.

Bashir is dividing pizzas to share with his friends.

Helpful Hint

A vertical line down OR a horizontal line across the center of a circle divides it into halves.

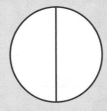

A vertical line down AND a horizontal line across the center of a circle divides it into fourths.

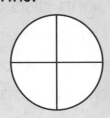

1. Bashir divides one pizza into halves. How many pieces will there be?

_____

2. Bashir divides a second pizza into fourths. How many pieces does he have?

_____

3. Are the halves of the same pizza the same size as the whole pizza?

_____

Are they the same shape as the whole pizza?

_____

Lesson 14.7 Shapes Practice

Read the problem carefully and solve. Show your work under each question.

Mr. Vaughn has students draw shapes on construction paper. Then, he has his students cut the shapes out.

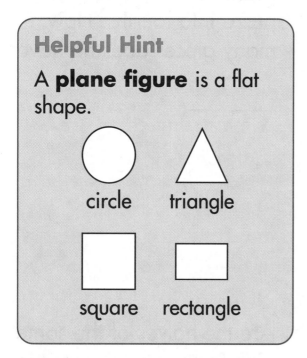

Helpful Hint

A **plane figure** is a flat shape.

circle   triangle

square   rectangle

1. Mr. Vaughn asks his students to draw squares. Draw a square below.

2. Mr. Vaughn has his students draw the plane figure shown below. How many sides does the figure have?

3. Mr. Vaughn also asks his students draw the plane figure shown below. How many square corners does the figure have?

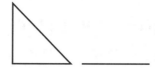

Check What You Learned

Recognizing and Drawing Shapes

Read the problem carefully and solve. Show your work under each question.

Mrs. Carson's class is having a bake sale.

1. Janetta brings in a chocolate cake. What shape is the top of it?

_____

2. Lior brings in cookies. What shape is the top of each cookie?

_____

3. Jake divides a circular cake into halves. How many pieces does he have?

_____

4. Annemarie brings in triangular cookies. How many sides does each cookie have?

_____ sides

Final Test Chapters 1–14

Read the problem carefully and solve. Show your work under each question.

Amy has 4 toy rabbits. The first rabbit is 12 inches tall. The second rabbit is 6 inches tall. The third rabbit is 36 inches tall. The fourth rabbit is 24 inches tall.

---

1. Which rabbit is 1 foot tall?

Rabbit #_____

3. How much taller is the third rabbit than the first rabbit?

_____ inches

2. Which rabbit is 1 yard tall?

Rabbit #_____

4. Amy has a box that is 18 inches tall. Which 2 rabbits will fit into Amy's box?

Rabbit #_____ and
Rabbit #_____

CHAPTERS 1–14 FINAL TEST

Spectrum Word Problems
Grade 2
100

Final Test
Chapters 1–14

Final Test Chapters 1–14

Read the problem carefully and solve. Show your work under each question.

Lacey is measuring leaves. She has a 3-inch leaf, a 5-inch leaf, and a 6-inch leaf.

1. Plot the length of each leaf on the number line.

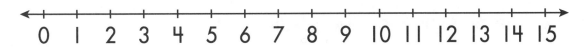

2. Lacey lays the 5-inch leaf next to the 3-inch leaf. How long are the leaves altogether? Plot the number on the number line.

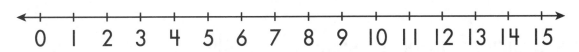

3. Lacey lays the 6-inch leaf next to the other 2 leaves. Now how long are the leaves altogether? Plot the number on the number line.

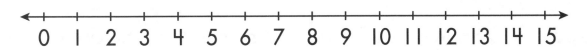

4. Lacey takes away the 5-inch leaf. Now how long are the leaves altogether? Plot the number on the number line.

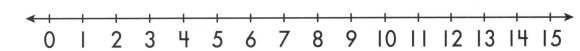

Spectrum Word Problems
Grade 2

Final Test
Chapters 1–14

101

CHAPTERS 1–14 FINAL TEST

Final Test Chapters 1–14

Read the problem carefully and solve. Show your work under each question.

Diego asked his friends what their favorite sports were. Their answers are in the table.

Soccer	Baseball
Soccer	Basketball
Basketball	Soccer
Baseball	Soccer

1. Draw a line plot showing the results.

2. Draw a picture graph showing the results.

3. Diego asks 2 more friends. One says baseball. The other says basketball. Draw a bar graph showing all the results.

CHAPTERS 1–14 FINAL TEST

Spectrum Word Problems
Grade 2
102

Final Test
Chapters 1–14

NAME _____

Read the problem carefully and solve. Show your work under each question.

Jeffrey is going to a concert. The concert starts at 8:15.

1. Show this time on an analog clock.

2. Show this time on a digital clock.

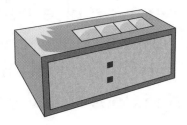

3. Jeffrey needs to leave for the concert at seven o'clock. Which clock shows the correct time?

4. The concert ends at 9:30. If it takes Jeffrey half an hour to get home, what time will he get home? Show the time on both clocks.

Spectrum Word Problems
Grade 2

CHAPTERS 1–14 FINAL TEST

Final Test
Chapters 1–14
103

Final Test Chapters 1–14

Read the problem carefully and solve. Show your work under each question.

Haley wants to buy some T-shirts. She has $20.00.

1. A black T-shirt costs $6.50. Haley buys 2 black T-shirts. How much money does she spend?

_____

3. Haley sells lemonade to earn more money. She makes this much money:

How much money does Haley earn?

_____

2. Next, Haley buys a red T-shirt. It costs $5.00. How much money does Haley have left?

_____

4. Haley buys a blue T-shirt. It costs $4.75. Haley gives the cashier $5.00. How much change does Haley get?

_____ cents

Spectrum Word Problems
Grade 2
104

CHAPTERS 1–14 FINAL TEST

Final Test
Chapters 1–14

Final Test Chapters 1–14

Read the problem carefully and solve. Show your work under each question.

Kelly is drawing shapes.

1. Kelly draws a pentagon. How many sides does it have?

   _____

3. Kelly draws a figure with 4 sides, but the sides are not equal. What shape does Kelly draw?

   _____

2. Kelly draws a hexagon. Draw a hexagon in the space below.

4. Kelly draws a circle. Then she divides it into fourths. Draw this figure in the space below.

Spectrum Word Problems
Grade 2

Final Test
Chapters 1–14
105

CHAPTERS 1–14 FINAL TEST

Scoring Record for Posttests, Mid-Test, and Final Test

Chapter Posttest	Your Score	Performance			
		Excellent	Very Good	Fair	Needs Improvement
1	___ of 4	4	3	2	1
2	___ of 4	4	3	2	1
3	___ of 4	4	3	2	1
4	___ of 4	4	3	2	1
5	___ of 4	4	3	2	1
6	___ of 4	4	3	2	1
7	___ of 4	4	3	2	1
8	___ of 4	4	3	2	1
9	___ of 4	4	3	2	1
10	___ of 4	4	3	2	1
11	___ of 4	4	3	2	1
12	___ of 4	4	3	2	1
13	___ of 4	4	3	2	1
14	___ of 4	4	3	2	1
Mid-Test	___ of 16	15–16	13–14	11–12	10 or fewer
Final Test	___ of 23	21–23	19–20	15–18	14 or fewer

Record your test score in the Your Score column. See where your score falls in the Performance columns. Your score is based on the total number of required responses. If your score is fair or needs improvement, review the chapter material.

Grade 2 Answers

Chapter 1

Pretest, page 1
1. 6
2. 14
3. 26
4. 16

Lesson 1.1, page 2
1. 8
2. 11
3. 19

Lesson 1.2, page 3
1. 5
2. 4
3. 2

Lesson 1.3, page 4
1. 25
2. 38
3. 26

Lesson 1.4, page 5
1. 67
2. 42
3. 30

Lesson 1.5, page 6
1. 98
2. 82
3. 95

Post-Test, page 7
1. 45
2. 49
3. 44
4. 52

Chapter 2

Pretest, page 8
1. red, black
2. blue, green
3. 12, even
4. 15, odd

Lesson 2.1, page 9
1. 8
2. 16
3. 24

Lesson 2.2, page 10
1. 6
2. 14
3. 20

Lesson 2.3, page 11
1. 11
2. 21
3. 32

Lesson 2.4, page 12
1. 8
2. 6
3. 12

Lesson 2.5, page 13
1. 16
2. 22
3. 15

Post-Test, page 14
1. 48
2. 18
3. 66
4. 20

Chapter 3

Pretest, page 15
1. 2
2. 9
3. 1
4. 7

Lesson 3.1, page 16
1. 100 + 7
2. 2
3. Marcus, 9

Lesson 3.2, page 17
1. 30
2. 5
3. 10

Lesson 3.3, page 18
1. 200
2. 1
3. 489

Lesson 3.4, page 19
1. 900
2. 400
3. 700

Grade 2 Answers

Lesson 3.5, page 20
1. 30
2. 40
3. 500

Lesson 3.6, page 21
1. Grade 4, 9
2. Grade 5, 8
3. Grade 1, 3

Post-Test, page 22
1. 100 + 50 + 2
2. Juan, 0
3. 20
4. Juan, 2

Chapter 4

Pretest, page 23
1. 100 + 20 + 3
2. 52 < 123
3. 1
4. 2

Lesson 4.1, page 24
1. 383
2. 419
3. George

Lesson 4.2, page 25
1. 1,000 + 200 + 80 + 3
2. 800 + 30 + 7
3. Mr. Smith's

Lesson 4.3, page 26
1. 1,038 > 684
2. 469 < 684
3. 684 = 684

Lesson 4.4, page 27
1. 400 + 80 + 5
2. 7
3. 485 < 652, Marissa

Post-Test, page 28
1. 1
2. 1,000 + 30 + 7
3. 1,037 < 1,142
4. 2,314

Chapter 5

Pretest, page 29
1. 728
2. 199
3. 176
4. 399

Lesson 5.1, page 30
1. 58
2. 95
3. 51

Lesson 5.2, page 31
1. 16
2. 24
3. 18

Lesson 5.3, page 32
1. 471
2. 803
3. 274

Lesson 5.4, page 33
1. 326
2. 201
3. 0

Lesson 5.5, page 34
1. 525
2. 209
3. 232

Post-Test, page 35
1. 615
2. 132
3. 202
4. 120

Chapter 6

Pretest, page 36
1. 116
2. 193
3. 31
4. 10

Lesson 6.1, page 37
1. 39
2. 52
3. 54

Grade 2 Answers

Lesson 6.2, page 38
1. 17
2. 8
3. 20

Lesson 6.3, page 39
1. 86
2. 118
3. 120

Lesson 6.4, page 40
1. 7
2. 9
3. 10

Lesson 6.5, page 41
1. 88
2. 94
3. 24

Post-Test, page 42
1. 157
2. 204
3. 20
4. No

Chapter 7

Pretest, page 43
1. 40
2. 500
3. 20
4. 227

Lesson 7.1, page 44
1. 30
2. 40
3. 50

Lesson 7.2, page 45
1. 200
2. 300
3. 800

Lesson 7.3, page 46
1. 40
2. 400
3. 60 flat rocks/210 curved rocks

Post-Test, page 47
1. 60
2. 90
3. 800
4. 900

Mid-Test

Page 48
1. 24
2. 16
3. 3
4. 4

Page 49
1. 6
2. 200
3. $100 + 30 + 1$
4. $100 < 205$

Page 50
1. 89
2. 161
3. 22
4. 31

Page 51
1. 64
2. 82
3. 8
4. 38

Chapter 8

Pretest, page 52
1. 6
2. 15
3. 4
4. 2

Lesson 8.1, page 53
1. 3
2. 2
3. 5

Lesson 8.2, page 54
1. 6
2. 15
3. 3 feet

Grade 2 Answers

Lesson 8.3, page 55
1. 6
2. 12
3. 2

Lesson 8.4, page 56
1. 12
2. 3
3. Yes

Post-Test, page 57
1. 3
2. Fly
3. 10
4. Measuring stick

Chapter 9

Pretest, page 58
1. 48
2. 11
3. 7
4. 7

Lesson 9.1, page 59
1. 15
2. 16
3. 7

Lesson 9.2, page 60
1. 24
2. 8
3. No

Lesson 9.3, page 61
1. 31
2. 41
3. 7

Post-Test, page 62
1. 9
2. 45
3. 21
4. 30

Chapter 10

Pretest, page 63
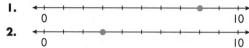

Lesson 10.1, page 64

Lesson 10.2, page 65

Lesson 10.3, page 66

Lesson 10.4, page 67

Post-Test, page 68

Chapter 11

Pretest, page 69–70

1.

			X		X	X	X				X		X	X
1	2	3	4	5	6	7	8	9	10	11	12	13	14	15

2.

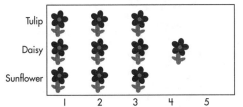

3.

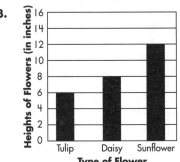

4.

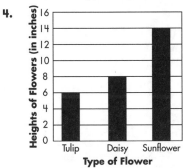

Lesson 11.1, page 71

1.

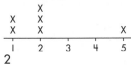

2. 2

3. 2

Lesson 11.2, page 72

1.

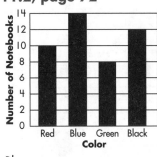

2. Blue

3. 4

Lesson 11.3, page 73

1.

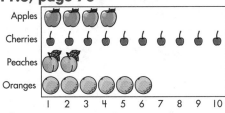

2. Cherries

3.

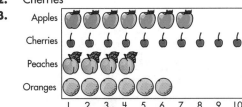

Lesson 11.4, pages 74–75

1.

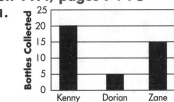

2.

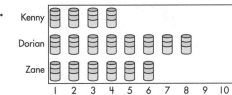

3.

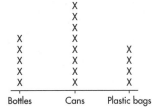

Grade 2 Answers

1.

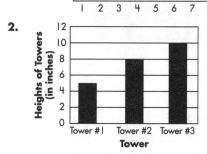

2.

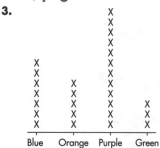

Post-Test, page 77

3.

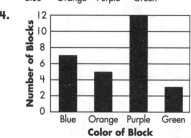

4.

Chapter 12

Pretest, page 78

1. 2:15
2. 3:45
3. 6:00
4. 4:00

Lesson 12.1, page 79

1.

2.

3.

Lesson 12.2, page 80

1. 8:00
2. 7:30
3. 10:00

Lesson 12.3, page 81

1.

2. 2:40
3. 3:00;

Lesson 12.4, page 82

1.

2. 9:00
3. Digital clock

Grade 2 Answers

Post-Test, page 83

1.

2. 7:00
3. 7:45
4. 7:00;

Chapter 13

Pretest, page 84

1. 2 dollars and 3 quarters
2. $7.65
3. 50 cents
4. 2 dollars and 10 cents

Lesson 13.1, page 85

1. 30, 6
2. 50, 5
3. 5, 95

Lesson 13.2, page 86

1. 3 dollars and 70 cents
2. 2 dollars and 50 cents
3. Evan has 7 dollars and 20 cents. Grace has 6 dollars and 0 cents.

Lesson 13.3, page 87

1. $13.75
2. $9.75
3. $3.25

Lesson 13.4, page 88

1. $3.00
2. $30.00
3. $4.00

Lesson 13.5, pages 89

1. $15.93
2. $19.93
3. $2.75

Post-Test, pages 90

1. $4.00
2. $8.00
3. $10.00
4. $18.00

Chapter 14

Pretest, pages 91

1. △
2. 0
3. 4
4.

Lesson 14.1, page 92

1. 1
2. 3
3. 3

Lesson 14.2, page 93

1. 4
2. 3
3. Square

Lesson 14.3, page 94

1. 3
2. 5
3. pentagon

Lesson 14.4, page 95

1. 6
2. 4
3. Square

Lesson 14.5, page 96

1.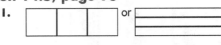
2.
3. Bigger

Lesson 14.6, page 97

1. 2
2. 4
3. No. No.

Lesson 14.7, pages 98

1.
2. 3
3. 1

Post-Test, page 99

1. Rectangle
2. Circle
3. 2
4. 3

Grade 2 Answers

Final Test, page 100
1. 1
2. 3
3. 24 inches
4. 1, 2

Final Test, page 101
1.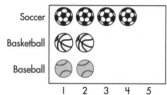
2.
3.
4.

Final Test, page 102
1.
```
X
X
X        X              X
X        X              X
Soccer  Basketball   Baseball
```

2.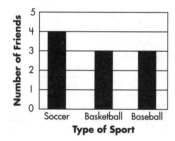

3.

Final Test, page 103
1.

2. 8:15

3.

4. 10:00;

Final Test, page 104
1. $13.00
2. $2.00
3. $3.95
4. 25 cents

Final Test, page 105
1. 5
2.

3. Rectangle
4.

Notes

Notes